Published by Golf Digest/Tennis, Inc.
A New York Times Company
495 Westport Avenue
P.O. Box 5350
Norwalk, Connecticut 06856

Trade book distribution by
Simon and Schuster, A Division
of Simon & Schuster, Inc.
Simon & Schuster Building
Rockefeller Center
1230 Avenue of the Americas
New York, New York 10020

First printing
ISBN: 0-914178-70-9
Library of Congress: 84-080549
Manufactured in the United States of America

Cover and book design
by Julie Francis
Printing and binding by
R.R. Donnelley & Sons

# ● MORE ●
# INSTANT
# TENNIS
# LESSONS

# ● MORE ●
# INSTANT
# TENNIS
# LESSONS

*Edited by Robert J. LaMarche*
*Illustrated by Elmer Wexler*
*A TENNIS Magazine Book*

# CONTENTS

# INTRODUCTION

If you're like most tennis players, you can probably recall a number of tennis tips from past instructors that still stand out in your mind because they really helped you improve. And the common thread that links all of them is simplicity. They are direct, concise pieces of advice and they evoke strong, graphic mental images that are easy to recall on court. Armed with these helpful pointers, you've been able to raise your level of play and avoid falling into bad stroking habits.

An aspiring tennis player can never get enough of these tips because he realizes there's always room for improvement. *More Instant Tennis Lessons* offers you just that—110 fully illustrated, attention-grabbing tips from some of the finest teaching pros in the game. Each of these mini-lessons has appeared in the pages of TENNIS magazine in recent years and has helped thousands of players like yourself strengthen different elements in their games. This book is intended to supplement the 84 proven tips contained in a first edition, *Instant Tennis Lessons*, which was published in 1978.

The private lessons found on the following pages are ideas that certified instructors, members of the United States Professional Tennis Association and the Professional Tennis Registry, have found to be especially effective in on-court lessons. As you look through *More Instant Tennis Lessons*, be selective in singling out tips to try in your next practice session. The idea is not to memorize each lesson that's presented, but to pick and choose. An instant lesson that works wonders for you, may not work as well for a friend.

Just consider, though, the incredible wealth of knowledge that's contained inside these covers. You owe it to yourself and your game to draw on that experience. Rapid improvement might be only a page or two away!

—*Robert J. LaMarche*

# 1
# SERVES

# BLOW OFF STEAM BEFORE YOU SERVE

The pressure and excitement of match play can exact a harsh toll on the server if he's not careful to vent his anxiety and relax before putting the next ball into play. That's because tension stiffens muscles. And a player who serves the ball with a tight, tense upper body usually has problems placing his delivery with accuracy and pace.

Pros with excellent serves take their time before beginning each point. You may have noticed that a lot of them take a deep breath and exhale as they step up to the baseline. That deep breath, like a water kettle venting the steam building inside it, releases pressure and relaxes the muscles in the upper body. So try blowing off steam before every serve. Your deliveries may become too hot for opponents to handle.

*—Don Henson*

# BOLT YOUR SHOE TO PREVENT FOOT FAULTS

Has an opponent ever caught you committing a foot fault? You couldn't believe it, right? The truth is, you can't say he made a bad call. If you're looking up at the ball the way you should during the service motion, it's almost impossible for you to detect a small movement of your front foot onto the baseline. And if you lift the toes of your front foot as you rock backward to establish a serving rhythm, you're particularly susceptible to committing foot faults.

One way to avoid foot-faulting is to pretend that the tip of the shoe placed nearest the baseline is bolted to the court. You'll still be able to pivot on the ball of your foot and transfer your weight properly. However, your toes will remain in contact with the ground. That will prevent you from taking a small step onto the line before you hit the ball and help you nail a legal serve.

—*Linda H. Winn*

# USE A PRE-FLIGHT CHECKLIST BEFORE LAUNCHING YOUR SERVES

Whenever club players head out on court to work on their serves, I notice that many of them end up perfecting their mistakes, rather than correcting them. They don't seem to take time to think about the service motion, opting instead to fire as many balls as possible across the net in the belief that a large number of serves alone will iron out their problems.

Your practice time should be used more wisely. Before each serve, you should go through a mental serving checklist, just as an airplane pilot reviews a pre-flight checklist before takeoff. Relax your muscles and focus your thoughts on making a good ball release and smooth service motion. If you practice in this constructive fashion, you'll probably discover your serving success in real matches will soar.

*—Brice Bassett*

# TUNNEL YOUR WAY TO ACCURATE SERVICE PLACEMENTS

Accurate placement, not raw power, is the key to serving effectively. Unfortunately, too many club players casually stride to the baseline, take a much-too-quick glance across the net and fire the ball without properly focusing their attention on a specific target area.

If you think you fit into this category of aimless players, slow down your serving tempo and concentrate on the placement of your delivery. Before you begin your service motion, visualize yourself standing in a tunnel that extends from your position at the baseline to the point where you want your serve to land. The tunnel will help you zero in on your target by blocking out all distractions around you, and its walls will help guide the ball straight to that spot. Use your tunnel vision to find the path to serving success.

*—Tom Dundis*

# START OFF EACH SERVE WITH A PENDULUM MOTION

Has anyone ever pointed out to you that your service motion looks stiff or mechanical? If they have, don't be offended. You should be grateful, because that person has spotted a flaw that could be seriously handicapping your serving efficiency. A stiff serving motion is a sure sign that you're tensing your muscles too much.

One way to help loosen up your delivery is to think of your hitting arm and racquet as a giant pendulum when you start your service motion. As you begin to lift the ball into the air, let the muscles in your hitting arm relax. Then, allow the weight of your racquet head to begin a smooth, uninhibited descending arc like a clock pendulum. Your arm shouldn't do any work in this phase of your delivery and that will help set up a fluid, relaxed service motion.

Remember to use the pendulum analogy and your opponent will have a tough time handling your serves.

*—Vic Brown*

# LIFT A WEIGHT FOR A MORE ACCURATE SERVICE RELEASE

One of the most common serving errors is a hurried ball release. Obviously, if you rush your release, you're more apt to flip the ball skyward, probably higher than necessary, in an inaccurate trajectory. And a hurried release will, in turn, force you to rush your racquet preparation and upward stroke in order to compensate. Add these problems together and you've got all the makings of a high-speed, slapstick comedy.

One way to slow down your service release is to imagine that a small weight is attached to your arm as you lift the ball in front of you. The imaginary weight will force you to raise your arm more deliberately and accurately. As a result, you won't have to rush your service motion to meet the ball solidly. If you remember to lift a weight on the release, your serves will become stronger.

—*Dave Kozlowski*

# LIFT THE BALL GENTLY, LIKE AN EGG, ON YOUR SERVICE RELEASE

If you're having difficulty placing the ball consistently and accurately on your service release, then you may be holding it too tightly in your fingers as you begin the service motion. That creates a stiffness in the hand and arm that can hamper the placement of your toss.

To remedy the problem, imagine that you're lifting an egg instead of a tennis ball as you start your delivery. Obviously, if you squeeze too hard, you're likely to end up with egg on your face. So the ball should rest on the tips of your fingers as you lift it gently upward. Then, when your hand reaches about head level, all you have to do is allow the ball to leave your fingertips naturally.

Your release will be more consistent and accurate. And the by-product should be a solid serve that sends opponents scrambling.
*—Mark Durham*

# SERVE UP A CUP OF COFFEE ON THE BALL RELEASE

Having trouble with your serve? Look to your ball release as a possible cause of your problems. Many club players, particularly in the late stages of a match when fatigue sets in, unknowingly alter their normal service release and flip the ball upward with a snap of the wrist. That makes it extremely difficult to place the ball consistently in the proper hitting zone.

Pretend the ball is a cup of hot coffee resting in your fingertips. To keep the coffee from spilling during your release, you'll have to lift your arm and hand smoothly, keeping your wrist steady. That way, the ball will leave your hand under control. So serve up some coffee to counteract late-match fatigue on your ball release.

— *Celeste Pregracke*

# FIND THE MISSING LINK IN YOUR SERVE

When you have one of those days when you can't seem to put a serve into play, resist the temptation to tinker immediately with your serving motion. First, examine your ball release because it's often the easily correctable culprit in serving problems.

To work on your ball release, you need go no farther than the corner of the chain-link fence surrounding your court. There, assume your normal serving stance about an arm's length away from the corner pole. Then, practice tossing the ball in the corner so that it doesn't flip back toward you or bounce off the pole. You can even select a level in the chain-link fence to serve as the maximum height for your release.

After practicing your release for a while, move back to the baseline to serve into the court. The chances are that you'll have found the missing link in your serving motion!

—*Marvin Rauchbach*

# TEE UP YOUR SERVES

Is your service toss too high? Do you have to time the upward swing of your service motion so that you meet the ball as it's descending? If that's the case, your serves probably lack consistency.

A solution to the problem is to think like a golfer who's preparing to hit a tee shot. He is allowed to place the ball on a wooden tee in order to keep it stationary. That way, he doesn't have to worry about adjusting his swing to hit a moving target.

Use that same principle when you serve. Imagine that you're teeing up the tennis ball with your service toss. Your goal is to lift the ball so that it peaks and hangs nearly motionless at the point where you can hit it with a full upward extension of your racquet, arm and body. When you're able to do that consistently, you can tee off on your serves with greater control.

—*Sara Hamilton*

# LIFT A WINDOW SHADE ON THE BALL TOSS

Your pro has probably told you how important it is to use a smooth, flowing service motion. And that advice applies not only to your hitting arm, but to your other arm as well—the one you use to toss the ball. A jerky ball release prevents you from placing the ball consistently in the proper hitting zone and throws off your timing.

You can correct the problem by imagining that you're lifting a window shade as you bring your arm up to release the ball. To raise a window shade so that it doesn't snap out of control, you would let your hand rise with the shade smoothly, until it was fully wound on the roller. That's how you should release the ball, too. Don't fling the ball in the air by stopping your hand and arm abruptly. Lift the ball smoothly in front and to the side of you as you would a window shade—and then let the ball leave your fingertips under control.

—*Gregg Kail*

# LIFT THE BALL UP A STOVEPIPE ON YOUR SERVE

You're at the baseline, ready to serve. You release the ball and it rises off-course. Yet you still try to hit it. The result? Your serve either sails long or slams into the net. Of course, you can cope with the problem by disciplining yourself to stop your swing after an errant toss, but that's not going to solve it. Instead, you should develop a consistent service release, one that puts the ball in the right place time after time. To do that, visualize an old-fashioned stove standing about a foot inside the baseline and just to your right if you're right-handed. During your service motion, release the ball so that it travels straight up the imaginary stovepipe to the spot where you want to make contact. With practice, your errant releases should virtually disappear.

*—Don Foster*

# PLACE THE BALL ON A SHELF FOR A GOOD SERVICE RELEASE

When players tell me they're having problems with their serves, one of the first things I look for as a cause is a faulty service toss. Actually, the word "toss" is partly to blame because it implies that you can use a quick, jerky motion to throw the ball into the air.

Instead, you should try to release the ball in a smooth lifting motion out in front and to the right of your body, if you're a right-hander. Visualize a shelf suspended above you, right at the point where you want to make contact with the ball. Now, place the ball there smoothly, lifting it gently so that it peaks just above the imaginary shelf and lands lightly on top of it. You should find that using a shelf image will provide an unlimited supply of more effective, consistent deliveries.

—*Gene Williams*

# REACH FOR AN ARROW ON THE SERVE

Tired of hitting soft, marshmallow serves? One of the keys to getting real power into your deliveries is to drop your racquet head behind you into what is commonly called a "back-scratching" position. It gives your arm and elbow the leverage that's needed to swing the racquet head quickly upward and generate the momentum you want when you hit the ball.

To get your racquet head in that position, imagine you're an archer who's reaching back to pull an arrow from a quiver strapped on your shoulder. How would you do it? First, you'd lift your elbow up and out from your body until it reached about shoulder height. Then, you'd drop your forearm and flex your wrist to grasp the end of the arrow.

Your arm should be in a similar position when you drop your racquet head behind you to serve. If you can incorporate that one element into your serving motion, then you'll help add power to your serve and make your opponents quiver.

—*Helen Wiley*

# FLEX YOUR LEG MUSCLES FOR STRONGER SERVES

When you have a chance, take a moment to watch the legs of the most effective servers in pro tennis during their serving motions. You'll notice that the pros have one thing in common: They flex their leg muscles just before they stretch up to hit the ball.

Many club players, in contrast, tend to serve while standing too stiff and upright. The upshot is a loss of power since the arm and shoulder are forced to do all of the work.

The next time you practice your serve, flex your legs as you drop the racquet head behind your back. This flexing action will allow you to use your leg muscles to spring upward and stretch out fully as you accelerate the racquet head through contact with the ball. Your serving motion should become more fluid and powerful.

So remember to flex your leg muscles if you really want to strengthen your serve.

*—Paul Gagon*

# ROTATE YOUR SHOULDERS LIKE A PITCHER

Have you ever watched the way a baseball pitcher winds up to throw a fastball? One of the key elements in his throwing motion is a distinctive shoulder rotation away from home plate, which helps to coil his upper body and store energy like a compressed spring.

That's one of the ways you can put more power into your serves on the tennis court, too. By the time you drop your racquet head behind your back in the serving motion, your shoulders should be coiled sideways, away from the net. Then, as you lean into the court and swing upward to hit the ball, you should rotate your shoulders forward to generate some extra momentum. With some experimentation and practice, you may be able to blow some balls past your opponent—the same way a fastball pitcher does.

*—Ron Vigneri*

# SERVE AT THE PEAK OF YOUR RELEASE

A ball release that's too high or too low is often to blame for many double faults. How can you correct the problem? It's simple. Serve a few dozen balls, disciplining yourself to swing at each one as it nears its peak—regardless of the ball's height. You'll probably whiff on a few and knock some others off the shaft of your racquet.

Don't be embarrassed, though. In just 15 minutes or so, the negative feedback that you get from your poor ball releases will automatically help you discover the optimum spot where you should place the ball. You'll learn to release the ball so it consistently peaks at a height where you can make good contact with a full upward extension of your body, arm and racquet. So remember, time your stroke to hit the ball at its peak. Your serving percentages will climb!

—*Tom Nelson*

# STRETCH LIKE A RUBBER BAND ON SERVES

It's a common sight at clubs everywhere: A player makes a good ball release on the serve, but waits for the ball to descend and hits it only a foot or two above head level. The result is a cramped, awkward-looking serving motion that produces a weak delivery.

If that describes too many of your serves, there's an easy way to correct the problem. And that is to remind yourself to stretch upward, like a rubber band, to meet the ball as far above head level as is comfortable for you. Don't wait for the ball to come down to you; use the spring in your legs and your full reach to go up after the ball aggressively. That way, you'll be able to put your whole body into your serve and generate better pace and depth.
—*Scott Andersen*

# PRACTICE SERVING BY THE BOOK

You need to tone up a number of different muscles—in the wrist, arm and shoulder—to serve as effectively as you can. Perhaps the best and easiest way to do that is to place a small book inside your racquet cover against the strings. Then, practice your service swing. The added weight at the head of the racquet, combined with greater air resistance created by the cover, should quickly strengthen those serving muscles.

*—Charles Tyrrell*

# OBEY A SPEED LIMIT ON SERVES

To insure that their second serves land in play, a lot of club players slow down their service motions and push the ball gently across the net. Of course, smart players capitalize on those marshmallow deliveries by moving in and punishing the ball.

If your second serves lack pace and depth, try to set a speed limit for your service motion and obey it for both first and second serves. Your forward swing on a second serve should be just as fast as for your first serve. The difference is that you should put more spin on your second serve to help bring the ball down into the service court. To do that, brush across the back of the ball instead of hitting through it squarely. So obey your speed limit and use spin to make your opponents respect your second serves.

*—Lewis M. Greer*

# REACH UP EXTRA INCHES FOR MORE SERVING POWER

Having trouble hitting your first serve in with power? Can't place it deep into the service box? One of the reasons why you've got a second-rate serve may be that you're not making contact with the ball far enough over your head. That can really rob you of power and accuracy.

For extra reach, use the spring in your legs and the uncoiling action of your body to extend yourself up into the air to hit the ball. During your motion, concentrate on extending your arm up higher, just a couple of inches, at impact and immediately afterward. You'll find that this extra reach, slight as it may seem, will accelerate the ball off your racquet strings faster and help you to follow through fully, giving you increased power and depth on your serve.

—*Paul Gagon*

# USE A HELPING HAND TO STEP UP YOUR SERVING POWER

If your serve lacks pace, you may not be transferring your weight forward during your service motion. A sure sign of a good weight transfer is a natural step forward into the court with your back foot as you hit the ball. Often, club players fail to take that momentum-generating step. Then, they must rely solely on arm strength to put pace on their serves.

To hit a more powerful serve, lean into the court as you reach up and swing out at the ball. Think of a giant hand gently pushing on your back. The pressure of that imaginary hand should force you to get your body weight moving forward by stepping into the court as you serve. And your step up in power will probably produce a handful of service winners each match.

*—Dean Snyder*

# REACH OUT TOWARD A TARGET WHEN YOU SERVE

Tennis pros everywhere will tell you that one of the most common serving errors is hitting down on the ball. Many inexperienced players mistakenly believe they must hit the ball with a downward trajectory in order to ensure its descent into the service court.

However, given the dimensions of the court and net, you'd have to be a giant to hit down on the ball so that it would clear the net and still land in play. The best way to add depth and pace to your serve is to reach up and out with your racquet arm as you stroke the ball toward an imaginary target positioned in the service court. That way, your racquet head will travel in the direction of the target longer and prevent a lot of netted deliveries. Your serves should begin to find their marks with much greater consistency.

*—Paul Gagon*

# CROSS YOUR ARMS ON THE FOLLOW-THROUGH FOR BETTER SERVES

Do your serves lack pace and accuracy? If they do, your timing and rhythm may be off. A common cause of this problem is the tendency to open the shoulders and hips toward the net too quickly before impact with the ball.

An easy way to check to see if you are making this serving error is to pause at the end of your follow-through and examine the position of your arms. If your free arm is behind your body, it's a sign that you've rotated your body too soon.

Instead, you should try to finish with your arms crossed in front of you, just to the side. That position indicates that you've kept your free arm up and out in front of you long enough to allow a properly timed shoulder turn. Remember, look to your follow-through if you want to cross-up opponents with tougher serves.

—*Andres Brandi*

# 2
# GROUND STROKES

# BATTER UP FOR BETTER PREPARATION

The next time you watch a professional tennis match, focus on one player and notice how quickly he takes his racquet back to prepare for the forward swing. On nearly every shot, he'll be well into his backswing by the time his opponent's returns have crossed the net. That's the key to hitting smooth, solid shots. If you wait until the ball bounces before you start the backswing, your stroke will be rushed and you'll lose control of the shot.

Think of the way a baseball batter gets ready to hit a pitch at home plate. He takes his bat back early, before the pitcher throws the ball, so that all he'll have to do is swing forward in an uncomplicated motion to make contact. Similarly, early racquet preparation should be your goal on the tennis court. Of course, you can't take your racquet back before your opponent sends back a return, but you should try to start your backswing early, just after contact has been made and you're able to determine the direction of his shot.

—*Joseph Pizzat*

# PREPARE EARLY FOR ONCOMING SHOTS

You've probably noticed this phenomenon on the highway. When it's in the distance, a car coming at you will appear to move slowly. But when it reaches you, the car is a blur of speed.

The same effect applies to balls hit straight at you on the tennis court. You aren't able to gauge their speed as easily as shots that come to you at an angle. As a result, you often make late contact.

What's the problem? Poor preparation, most likely. Unlike balls directed crosscourt, shots hit right at you don't move laterally against a fixed background. Without the visual reference guide, their velocities can be extremely deceptive—like the cars coming at you on the highway. But you can cope with deceptive ball speeds by making sure to prepare your racquet early. That way, you should be able to make contact out in front of your body and drive the ball solidly across the net.

—*Patrick Mason*

# BE PREPARED! TURN YOUR SHOULDER IMMEDIATELY

Do you frequently find yourself hitting the ball late on ground strokes, sending the ball across the sidelines and into a neighboring court? It's pretty embarrassing, isn't it? You can correct the problem by disciplining yourself to take the racquet back early so you don't have to rush your forward swing. The key to this good racquet preparation is to turn your shoulders sideways to the approaching ball immediately after you determine whether it's coming to your forehand or backhand. Imagine that you're being timed by a stopwatch and begin rotating your shoulders a split second after your opponent hits the ball. By quickening your reaction time this way, you'll be able to concentrate better on your forward stroke and meet the ball in front of your body.

—*Michael Duvall*

# POINT AT THE BALL WITH YOUR RACQUET HANDLE

When your usually reliable ground strokes begin slamming into the net or flying out of bounds like errant missiles, check to make sure that you're starting your backswing early enough. In the heat of battle, you may forget the basics of good stroking and wait for your opponent's shot to land in your court before taking your racquet back. But late racquet preparation, of course, forces you to rush your forward stroke and exacts a harsh toll in terms of control.

Instead, start your backswing early enough so that your racquet handle points almost directly at the approaching ball before it bounces. That way, you won't have to rush your shot; with your racquet already back, you can take a smooth, controlled forward swing that will help set your ground strokes straight.

*—Larry Abrams*

# ADJUST THE HEIGHT OF YOUR BACKSWING

When you take your racquet back in preparation to hit a ground stroke, do you adjust the level of your backswing to match the height of the ball's bounce? You should. If an underspin ball bounces toward you, for example, it's going to stay very low in the court. And if you've taken a high backswing, at about shoulder level, then there's little chance of your making a good return. In fact, the ball will probably travel straight into the net. So on all shots, regardless of the type of spin that your opponent puts on the ball, try to adjust the height of your racquet on the backswing. By keeping it at roughly the same level as the ball after it bounces, you should make solid contact.

—*Fred Pinho*

# WALK THE RAILS FOR CONSISTENCY

Many players have difficulty getting into a good hitting position for ground strokes, especially after running wide to the left or right to intercept a shot. That's often because they either overrun the shot or stop too far away from the proper point of contact. In both cases, the results are the same: loss of power and accuracy. To help correct the problem, visualize a railroad track in your half of the court, parallel with the sidelines. As you near the line of flight of the ball, position yourself on one imaginary rail and reach out comfortably to meet the ball so that the point of contact is above the opposite rail. Try not to step on the imaginary ties between the rails. You'll find that this concept will improve your space perception and ability to judge distances—leading to more consistent strokes.

*—Joseph Pizzat*

# KEEP YOUR HEAD STILL, LIKE A GOLFER, THROUGH CONTACT

One of the leading causes of mis-hit ground strokes is a sudden, often unnoticed, movement of the head just before contact with the ball. This movement hampers your ability to track an approaching ball into your hitting zone and disturbs your balance.

If you've ever played golf, you know how disastrous a premature lifting of the head can be in terms of control. Usually, you'll shank the ball off to the side. In tennis, it's just as important to keep your head stationary through contact because you have to hit a moving ball, not one that's sitting motionless on a tee.

Remember: To drive your shots the length of the court with greater accuracy, keep your head down like a golfer and your eyes focused on the ball through contact.

*—Teeter Johnston*

# PRESS AND LIFT FOR TOPSPIN GROUND STROKES

Many club players hit the ball too flat and hard, resulting in low trajectory shots that lack control and often sail beyond the baseline or slam into the net. The secret of hitting consistent, controlled and powerful ground strokes lies in using topspin to make the ball clear the net by a safe margin and bring it down quickly into the opposite court. You can get a feel for this topspin by holding a ball against the center strap of the net with the head of your racquet. To make the ball go over the net, press firmly and lift the racquet face up the back of the ball. The next time you hit a ground stroke, swing from low to high and at impact imagine that you're pressing and lifting the ball back over the net.

*—Dave Kozlowski*

# SPIN A WHEEL FOR TOPSPIN GROUND STROKES

If too many of your forehand and backhand drives are finding the tape and dropping back onto your side of the court, it's time to add some topspin to your stroking attack in order to give your shots greater clearance over the net.

Here's a way to get that topspin: Imagine that you're trying to spin a bicycle wheel as you bring your racquet up to the ball. To do that, you would swing on a gradually rising path, from low to high, and brush the top half of the imaginary wheel with your racquet's bow to make the wheel spin away from you rapidly. That's the type of stroking motion you need to impart topspin to the ball.

So visualize that wheel the next time you're on the court and you'll soon send topspin shots sailing well above the net.

—*John Davis*

# LET YOUR RACQUET RIDE AN ESCALATOR ON GROUND STROKES

A flat, roundhouse type of swing on ground strokes is a tip-off to an opponent that you're not likely to stay in baseline rallies for long. Your flat shots will catch the net more often than not and your circular swing will make accurate placements nearly impossible.

To shore up your erratic ground game, add some natural topspin to your forehand and backhand. How? Imagine that your racquet head is riding an escalator upward on your forward stroke. A rising stroking path and a vertical racquet face at impact will impart the topspin necessary to give your shots greater clearance over the net.

And just as importantly, moving your racquet head along the straight line of an imaginary escalator through contact will provide better control. That's because your racquet will remain aligned with your target for a split-second longer than it would on a roundhouse swing. So take an escalator to lift your ground game to new heights!

—*Daniel Schrank*

83

# LEVEL OFF ON HIGH-BOUNCING BALLS

Whenever you face an opponent who hits with heavy topspin, you're likely to have to return a number of high-bouncing balls from behind your baseline. In those situations, you should resist the urge to use your normal slice or topspin strokes. Why? A slice return from shoulder level or higher is difficult to time and increases the risk of hitting a ball that catches the net. And it's virtually impossible to return a high ball with any pace if you attempt a topspin stroke.

Instead, your best bet is to use a level swing. Imagine there's a carpenter's level extending through the point of contact and keep your racquet head on that same plane during your stroke. Because the ball is above shoulder height, a level swing will permit you to drive the ball deep with plenty of clearance over the net.

—*Tom Nelson*

# FOLLOW THROUGH ON A PEDESTAL

Are you frequently off balance after hitting a ground stroke? Do you have trouble getting back into your ready position? If you do, you're most likely taking a gargantuan swing and finishing with an awkward follow-through.

One solution to this problem is to imagine that you're standing on a pedestal that's just big enough to allow you to step into the ball as you make your swing. That should force you to use a more controlled stroke and finish with a natural, flowing follow-through; otherwise, you'd fall off your high perch. So put yourself on a pedestal when you hit ground strokes.

—*Gary Horvath*

# TAKE OFF ON YOUR GROUND STROKES!

Do too many of your ground strokes slam into the net? If they do, you're not giving the ball enough vertical lift to clear the net safely. You're probably hitting the ball with a forward swing that's too flat. To correct the problem, concentrate instead on using a gradually ascending forward stroke.

Imagine that your racquet head is following the path of a jet as it takes off from an airport runway. Start your racquet on a "runway" below the level of the approaching ball and swing it forward with steadily increasing speed. Climb gradually, like the jet, to meet the ball and then let the racquet head continue through the hit and move outward in the direction of the shot. That way, you'll get better ball clearance over the net, allowing you to stay in points longer.

*—Lucky Cotten*

# KICK UP YOUR HEELS FOR DEEP GROUND STROKES

If your ground strokes fall consistently short in the other court, look to your forward weight transfer as a possible cause of your problem. You're probably trying to rely on arm strength alone to supply enough power to send your drives deep. But you can't do that.

Instead, you must step into your shots, so your body weight is moving forward, in order to get the depth you need. To check your weight transfer, freeze on your follow-through during practice and see if the heel of your back foot is lifted slightly off the ground. It should be if you've shifted your weight forward properly. So kick up your heels to get the depth you need on your ground strokes.

—*Barry Goldsmith*

# POSE ON YOUR FOLLOW-THROUGH

When they're engaged in a rally from the baseline, many club players get so anxious about preparing for their next shot that they forget to follow through completely on the shot they're in the process of making. And that, of course, can have disastrous effects in terms of depth and placement.

On ground strokes, it's vital to follow through fully in the direction you've hit the ball; the racquet head must finish high out in front of your body. To be sure that you're finishing your stroke that way, hold a pose for a second, as though you were having your photo taken, at the end of your follow-through. Use that small fraction of time to check your racquet position in front of you. You'll find that a full follow-through—and the control you'll get from it—will pose big problems for opposing players.

—*Samuel L. Giles*

# KEEP YOUR HEAD DOWN TO AVOID TELEGRAPHING YOUR SHOTS

Do your opponents seem to have an uncanny ability to anticipate the direction of your shots? If they do, you may be telegraphing your shot-placement intentions unknowingly.

And you're not alone. A lot of club players virtually hand points to their opponents because of one simple mistake: They pick up their heads slightly at contact and glance quickly in the direction they're trying to hit the ball. Smart opponents, of course, will get the message and move immediately in that direction.

The next time you play, concentrate on keeping your head down and your eyes fixed on the point of impact for a second or two after the ball leaves your racquet. That way, you won't give your opponent as many messages that he can use to head off your shots.

*—Chuck Moore*

# SWING DOWN A CORRIDOR

When things start to get tight in a match, when your back is up against the wall, does your ground-stroke control tend to go haywire? If it does, the problem may be that the pressure is leading you to crank up for your shots with huge, inefficient swings.

To remedy the problem, imagine you are standing in a corridor and that your back is up against a real wall when you start your backswing. The wall should prevent you from taking too large a backswing and finishing with too long a follow-through.

The other corridor wall should be a comfortable distance in front of you, permitting you to make contact with the ball using a natural stroking motion, not one that's cramped or overextended.

Remember, confine your swing to a corridor; that will help keep your ground strokes clean, crisp and effective.

*—Mike O'Connell*

# PRETEND THE NET'S A WALL

Do your ground strokes always seem to clear the painted net line on a practice backboard by a safe margin, but find the net once you step onto a real tennis court?

The transparent nature of the net may be responsible for your problem. From the baseline, you can look through the net and see the boundary lines in your opponent's half of the court. And the sight of those lines may tempt you to hit a lower shot to make sure that the ball doesn't sail out of bounds.

To help solve that problem, pretend that the net is actually a solid brick wall. Or drape a couple of old blankets over the net to block your view of the opposite court. Now, rally for several minutes with a practice partner, swinging on a slightly upward path to hit your ground strokes. You should find it easy to groove shots that will clear the net-wall safely.

—*Michael Owens*

# RALLY IN AN ALLEY TO IMPROVE ACCURACY

Can you place your ground strokes accurately enough to wear down an opponent during a long baseline-to-baseline exchange? A great way to improve your shot placement so you can outsteady a player in those ground stroke duels is to make good use of a doubles alley in your practice sessions.

The next time you work on your game, move over into the alley with your practice partner after your warm-up period. Then, exchange ground strokes within the doubles alley. Count how many times you can successively trade shots in bounds and play a few points, too, using only the doubles alley as your target. You'll soon discover that the small dimensions of the alley will force you to be a lot more precise with your ground stroke placement. And that, in turn, should help you run your opponents ragged in a match.

—*Paul Gagon*

# REACH OUT FOR SUCCESS ON YOUR FOREHAND

Do you have trouble controlling your forehand? Does your swing ever feel cramped or do your shoulders open prematurely during the stroke? Poor racquetwork, of course, could be the problem. But your nonhitting arm might be the real culprit if you tend to let it hang down by your side as you make your stroke.

Your free arm, when used properly, helps you maintain your balance, make a better weight transfer and complete your follow-through. The next time you practice your forehand, try reaching out for approaching balls with your free arm. This simple movement should help eliminate cramped swings and keep your shoulders turned sideways during the stroke.

Remember, let your free arm lend you a hand in hitting solid forehands.

—*Kenneth P. Wasserman*

# POINT YOUR SHOULDER TO GO DOWN THE LINE

Do you feel you can always rely on your forehands down the line? Or do your attempts usually sail too wide or too far toward the center of your opponent's baseline? The shot, obviously, calls for accurate placement because the target area down the line is smaller than it is on a crosscourt forehand.

One important key to developing that accuracy is proper shoulder rotation during your backswing. You should always try to pivot your upper body so that your front shoulder points down the sideline where you're aiming. This alignment, combined with a good stance in which your feet are also squared off to the sideline, will make it much easier for you to place the ball accurately.

—*Fred Pinho*

# SLIDE A PATIO DOOR FOR SOLID FOREHANDS

Are you spraying your forehands all over the court? You may be using a stroking motion that's too circular. If that's the case, the slightest error in timing can cause the ball to fly off your racquet at an extreme angle.

You can improve your accuracy appreciably by swinging so that your racquet strings face the intended target area across the net for as long as possible before and through contact with the ball. Try laying back your hand and wrist slightly as you make your stroke—much as you would if you were sliding open a patio door.

That way, you'll find it much easier to keep your racquet head traveling along a straighter, truer path through contact with the ball. The result, of course, will be increased accuracy. And it should open the door to more wins on the court.

—*Leo Vorwerk*

# HIT AN AERIAL APPROACH SHOT OFF A HIGH FLOATER

You've almost surely been taught to take advantage of a short return by hitting an approach shot and advancing to the net. But what should you do when you have an opponent winded during a point and he hits a high, deep floater back to you?

Most club players will take a few steps back and hit the ball after the bounce, near the back fence. That tactic, though, could cost you the point. By moving back, you not only give your opponent a chance to regain his composure; you also allow him to take the offensive because he knows you can't do much harm from so deep in your backcourt.

What you should do is to move in and take the ball on the fly by hitting an aerial approach shot. Use a compact volley-type motion, meet the ball solidly before it bounces and drive it deep into a corner of the opposite court. Then, follow your aerial approach to the net and wait for the weak return you can put away for a winner!

—*Dave Kozlowski*

# THINK THUMB AND HIP FOR BACKHANDS

If you're having trouble hitting a solid, consistent backhand, you may be preparing for the shot with your arm and elbow extended too far away from your body. With your arm floating out like that, it's impossible for you to swing the racquet forward fluidly to make contact with the ball.

There's an easy way to correct the problem, though. As you take your racquet back behind you, think about trying to touch your rear hip with the thumb of your racquet hand. By the time you complete your backswing, this thought should automatically position your arm and elbow close to your body—a point from which you'll be able to swing forward smoothly. The result? Greater power, control and consistency on your backhands.

*—Paul Gagon*

# CONTROL YOUR ELBOW FOR SOLID BACKHAND APPROACH SHOTS

The sight of a short ball coming across the net gives most players a shot of adrenaline during a rally. Unfortunately, that extra excitement sometimes makes it difficult to execute a smooth, controlled stroke in launching an approach shot. On the backhand side, in particular, the elbow tends to extend outward too far from the body, severely reducing any chance of placing the ball accurately.

The key to hitting a solid backhand approach shot is to control your elbow by keeping it tucked in toward your rib cage at a comfortable distance from your body. Relax during the stroke and don't allow your elbow and racquet to move out of your control zone. That way, you'll be able to channel your extra energy into hitting a putaway volley at the net a few seconds later.

*—Denny Schackter*

# SLOW DOWN IN YOUR TRACKS TO HIT AN APPROACH SHOT

In their eagerness to move in on short balls and reach the net, many club players run full tilt from the backcourt, like a speeding train. The results are often wild, rushed approach shots that crash into the net.

Sound familiar? While it's a good idea to advance to the net as quickly as possible when an opportunity presents itself, you've got to execute a smooth, accurate approach shot or else you'll waste your effort. Your initial movement to reach a short ball should be quick. But as you prepare to make contact, you should slow your momentum, like a train traveling up a steep grade. That will allow you to hit the ball with depth and accuracy toward your target. After impact, you can pick up speed to get closer to the net. Train yourself to slow down on approach shots to keep your offensive game on track.

—*Christopher Bradley*

115

# OPEN THE DOOR TO BETTER BACKHAND APPROACH SHOTS

Do your backhand approach shots often fall short in your opponent's court, allowing him to step in and crack blistering passing shots for winners? If that happens to you a lot, you may be leaning back as you make contact with the ball.

A good way to correct the problem is to imagine you're trying to free a jammed door that has been swollen shut by dampness. By doing that, when you hit the shot, you'll keep your front shoulder down and lean forward. You'll be using your forward momentum to add pace and depth to your approach shot. And you'll keep your opponent on the defensive.

Remember, use your forward momentum to open the door to success at the net.

*—Lee Holmes*

# SLIDE INTO THOSE SLICED BACKHAND APPROACH SHOTS

Some club players chop at the ball when they attempt a sliced backhand approach shot and, as a result, knock it into the net. If you've been getting similar results lately, you should take measures to guarantee a smoother, more fluid stroke.

One way you can do that is to imagine that you're moving your racquet head steadily down a playground slide as you swing to meet the ball. Start your racquet head above the level of the planned point of impact and let it slide down, hit the ball and finish below that point, out in the direction of your target.

That high-to-low forward stroking motion, combined with a good weight transfer to your front foot, will combine to produce a shot with underspin that should force your opponent to hit a rising shot, which you can pounce on to end the point.

*—Bill Delaney*

# FINISH THUMBS-UP FOR TOPSPIN BACKHANDS

Do your flat or slice backhands tend to catch the net a bit too often? Then you should consider adding topspin to your backhand ground attack.

To do that, you'll have to break your routine of using a relatively flat or downward stroke. Instead, you should bring your racquet forward on a rising path to impart the topspin that will give your backhands plenty of clearance over the net and a good kick on the bounce. One simple way to groove the necessary low-to-high stroke (if you use an Eastern backhand grip) is to concentrate on finishing your swing with your thumb pointing in an upward direction on the handle. That kind of follow-through will help ensure that you've accelerated your racquet head in an upward brushing motion through contact with the ball. So use a thumbs-up follow-through to produce reliable topspin backhands.

*—Rick Macci*

# 3

# VOLLEYS

123

welur

# PROTECT THE NET LIKE A HOCKEY GOALIE

Every time you advance to the net, you increase your offensive potential. But your primary task up there, if you think about it, is essentially a defensive one: You have to guard against your opponent's passing shot attempts and keep your eyes open for deep lobs, too.

In fact, your role at the net is similar in some ways to that of a hockey goalie who must defend his net. Consider how a goalie performs his job: He moves to cut down opponents' angles of attack, stays on the edges of his skates and crouches slightly, ready to spring in any direction to block a flying puck.

You should use the same principles to protect the net in a tennis match. Always position yourself to cut down an opponent's angle of attack. And, of course, keep your weight forward, poised to intercept passing shot attempts and ready to run down lobs. If you do that, you'll even be one up on a hockey goalie— you'll be able to score points, too!

—*Chuck Davis*

# FENCE YOUR WAY TO BETTER NET PLAY

Net play in club matches often tends to resemble scenes from old Errol Flynn swashbuckling movies. Players wave their racquets around like huge, unwieldy swords with uncontrolled swings.

While it's certainly advantageous to be aggressive at the net, you should always try to keep your racquet head under control. Instead of playing the net like a swashbuckler, you should adopt the more disciplined style of a fencer who keeps the tip of his foil up and out in front of him, ready to parry his opponent's thrusts with short, quick movements.

When you're at the net, keep your racquet head cocked up in front of you. That way, you'll be able to react more quickly and move into the compact volleying motion that should foil your opponent's passing shot attempts.

—*James Lathrop*

# PLAY A CHILD'S PADDLE GAME FOR A WINNING VOLLEY

If you enjoy playing an aggressive style of tennis but have trouble ending points at the net, you should check on whether you're trying to do too much, too quickly with your volleys. In other words, you should make sure you cut back on big swings that are difficult to time.

Here's how. As a child, do you remember playing with those wooden paddles that had rubber balls attached to them with rubber bands? In order to keep the ball rebounding off the paddle continuously, you had to use very short, compact stroking motions. If you tried to take a big swing at the ball, you usually missed it or the next shot completely.

Keep that in mind when you volley in tennis. Paddle the ball firmly, but keep your motion compact. You'll feel like a kid at the net!

—James Alletto

# YOUR GATEWAY TO BETTER VOLLEYS

The volley, whether forehand or backhand, is a stroke that must be kept compact in order for it to be effective. So if you've been having problems with your volleys, check to make sure that you're not overswinging at the ball. An easy way to do that is to stand directly beneath the entrance gate to a tennis court and have a friend toss a ball to your forehand and backhand sides. If your backswing is too long, you'll soon find that the racquet head will strike the metal gate post with a resounding "clang" as you turn your shoulders to prepare for the hit. Let that noise be a reminder every time you go to the net to use a short backswing and to punch forward and through the ball.

—*Ray Smith*

# GUN DOWN VOLLEYS AT EYE LEVEL

If you've ever shot a gun or watched a sharp-shooting event, you know that the best way to hit a target is to bring the weapon up to eye level so that you can take aim down the gun barrel. A shot from the hip, obviously, cannot be as accurate.

The same principle applies when you're playing the net. Why? In order to hit volleys on target, you should meet the ball with your racquet as close to eye level as possible. On volleys below your waist, for example, you'll sacrifice a great deal of control if you simply drop your racquet head and remain standing upright.

Instead, you should bend at the knees to bring your upper body, head and eyes closer to the level of the ball. From this position, you can more easily set your sights on the approaching ball, make solid contact and gun down your opponent!

—*Stanton Singer*

# STRETCH OUT LIKE A FIRST BASEMAN ON VOLLEYS

Few situations in tennis are as frustrating as blowing an easy putaway volley after carefully working your way to the net during a long rally. Often, a late hit is responsible for your error; you take a backswing that's too long and allow the ball to get almost past you before contact.

The key to hitting a solid, crisp volley is to meet the ball out in front of your body so that you can use your weight to generate pace on the shot. Otherwise, your arm is forced to do all of the work.

Think of yourself as a first baseman in baseball. On a close play at first, you'd have to stretch out to catch the ball before the runner reached the base. You should do the same thing at the net: Be aggressive and meet the ball out in front of your body. That way, you'll cut down on your backswing and put away your opponents quickly.

*—Brice Bassett*

# PUSH THE LEATHER FOR SOLID, ACCURATE VOLLEYS

Take a quick glance around your club's courts and you're likely to see a number of players in the forecourt, volleying balls as if they were swatting at flies. They don't realize how tough it is to control the placement of the ball with those kind of swinging volleys.

If a lot of your volleys have been off target lately, you may be using too much racquet-head motion yourself. The cure? Concentrate on keeping your wrist firm and simply pushing your leather racquet grip forward through contact, toward a target in your opponent's court. This clean motion should effectively eliminate any slapping tendencies. So remember to push the leather on your volleys to put pressure on your opponents.

*—Howard ("Curly") Davis*

# STRETCH A SPRING ON YOUR BACKHAND VOLLEY

Have you ever noticed how crisp and compact the top pros keep their backhand volleying motions? They eliminate all unnecessary movement from their strokes. That's what gives them superb control and accurate placement.

Your backhand volleys can be just as crisp and compact. Imagine that the ends of a tight spring are attached to the throat of your racquet and the hand you use to cradle your racquet in the ready position. After you pivot sideways and start your racquet forward to meet the ball, your imaginary spring will stretch out only a short distance, preventing you from taking a huge swing.

Then, the spring will help draw your free hand back to the racquet throat quickly so you'll be prepared for your next shot. Remember to use your spring to snap up points when you're at the net.

*—Jefferson T. Barnes*

# SQUARE UP TO HIT LOW VOLLEYS

How consistent are your low volleys at the net?
Do you send far too many sailing out of
bounds? If that's the case, you're probably dropping the racquet head below the level of your
wrist to hit the ball, which means you have to
use a scooping motion that's difficult to control.

To correct the problem, imagine there's a
carpenter's square between your racquet and
the court surface each time you hit a low
volley. Your objective is to keep your racquet
head above wrist level and never let it drop
below the parallel line formed by the top edge
of the carpenter's square. To do that, you'll
have to flex your entire body, especially at the
knees, to get down to the level of the ball.
Remember, square up your racquet to hit low
volleys and you'll keep the pressure on your
opponent.

*—Dean Snyder*

# BEND FOR LOW VOLLEYS LIKE A SKATEBOARDER

You think you're bending down far enough to hit low volleys at the net, but your shots too often are weak pop-ups. What's wrong? Chances are you're bending only at the waist to reach the ball. That type of stiff bending action doesn't allow you to move or react quickly enough to return low balls in the forecourt. All you can do is drop your racquet head and hit a slow, rising, off-balance volley.

To solve the problem, imagine you're on a skateboard. A person who's adept at riding a skateboard knows that the trick to maintaining good balance and coordination is to keep the body's center of gravity low by bending at the knees and the waist. You should flex your body in similar fashion to hit low volleys. By doing that, you'll be poised to go on a roll at the net!

—*Joseph Kamrad*

# USE YOUR RACQUET AS A SHIELD TO DEFLECT TOUGH VOLLEYS

When you're at the net and a ball is drilled directly at you from close range, quick reactions and proper racquet work are your only protection. Too often, however, inexperienced players will simply cringe and shy away from the ball or try to make contact by using a forehand volley only a contortionist could love.

The best way to protect yourself and return the ball in such a situation is to use your racquet as a shield, just as ancient warriors used to ward off blows from attackers with their shields. A little experimentation with your racquet off the court should prove to you that you can more effectively protect your entire body with a backhand reflex volley. Simple arm and hand movements and a firm grip at contact are all that's necessary to shield your body and deflect your attacker's shot. Do that, and you'll still be in the battle!

—*James V. Dorrell*

# GIVE THE "SAFE" SIGNAL ON BACKHAND VOLLEYS

A common flaw in many club players' backhand volleys is their tendency to chop down on the ball, allowing the racquet head to drop below wrist level. Usually, the result is a volley hit off-balance with so little pace and control that it catches the net.

To hit a more effective backhand volley, keep your wrist firm and, instead of chopping down on the ball, flatten out your volleying motion. Think of yourself as a baseball umpire giving a "safe" signal when you hit the ball. As you punch forward on your volley, your free arm should extend away from your body simultaneously in the opposite direction to help you maintain your balance and keep your volleying motion crisp and compact.

By hitting "safe" and sure backhand volleys, you'll find yourself scoring more often at the net.

—*Don Harring*

# LISTEN TO YOUR HALF VOLLEYS

If you have difficulty hitting consistent half volleys, your problem may be that you're not hitting the ball immediately after it bounces. These shots become increasingly more difficult to play when you let the ball rise more than a few inches off the court surface. To learn to hit the ball more quickly after the bounce, pay more attention to the sounds associated with the shot: the sound of the ball bouncing on the court and the sound of the ball meeting your racquet at impact. When you hit a proper half volley, these sounds should immediately follow each other in a brief staccato burst. So listen to your half volleys and watch your shot improve.

—*Chet Murphy*

# FIELD HALF VOLLEYS ON THE SHORT HOP

If you're like a lot of club players, you probably don't have much confidence in your half volley. As a result, you may tend to stiffen up and shy away from returns that are hit at your feet.

The key to hitting solid half volleys is to get down low to the ball and meet it immediately after it bounces. In fact, you should go after the ball on a half volley in much the same way as a baseball infielder aggressively moves in on a bouncing ground ball to take it on a short hop. Rather than stay back and risk getting a bad bounce, the smart infielder takes charge of the play.

So the next time you get a low ball at your feet, don't back away. Instead, move up and hit your half volley on the short hop.

—*Daniel Schrank*

# FEATHER YOUR DROP VOLLEYS AT THE NET

Hitting a successful drop volley requires a lot of touch and finesse. It's tough to stand at the net and try to hit a drop volley off a hard passing shot attempt. If you use a firm wrist and simple blocking action, the chances are that the ball will rebound off your strings and land deep enough in the opposite court to give your opponent time to make a return.

In order to take the pace off a hard-hit shot, you must relax your grip and arm at contact. Think of your racquet as a giant feather and lightly caress the ball over the net. Your racquet and arm should give slightly upon impact to allow you to drop the ball softly in your opponent's forecourt. If you practice feathering your drop volleys with finesse, you'll find your light touch will take a heavy toll on opposing players.

*—Dave Kozlowski*

# BUNT YOUR DROP VOLLEYS

In baseball, a surprise bunt that's hit by a batter when the infielders are playing deep can really shake up the defense. In tennis, the shot that has the same effect is the drop volley.

When you're in command of a point at the net and you have your opponent pinned deep behind the baseline, you can occasionally try to take the pace off his passing shot attempts and drop a volley softly over the net, out of his reach.

Like a baseball player who lays down a surprise bunt, loosen your grip slightly on the racquet just before impact to take the velocity off your opponent's shot and lift the ball over the net. Of course, your opponent will catch on if you use the shot too often. But if you can bunt a drop volley for a winner now and then, you'll have a major-league weapon.

—*Gary Miller*

# 4

## LOBS

157

# DRIVE YOUR LOBS FOR CONTROL

If you're often hitting lobs that fly beyond the baseline, you may not be following through sufficiently on the shot. The lob is actually a drive hit high into the air and it demands as much sustained contact between the racquet and ball as possible. So if you bring your swing to a screeching halt as you contact the ball, you're sacrificing contol by allowing the ball to bounce erratically off of the strings of your racquet. Remember, when you complete your swing, your racquet head should finish well above your head. This extended follow-through will help you place the ball more precisely in your opponent's court.

*—Dan Campbell*

# BUY TIME WITH DEFEN-SIVE LOBS

When a tough opponent sends you scrambling madly for a deep, wide drive, you must beware of the temptation to thread the needle with a passing shot. Why? By the time you reach the ball, you'll probably be out of position—not to mention out of breath—making it extremely difficult for you to put any mustard on your shot.

The wise play in this situation is to send up a defensive lob, deep enough to force your opponent to retreat toward his own baseline. The high, arcing trajectory of the shot will allow you to buy some valuable time, so you can get back into good position and catch your breath.

—*Gary Horvath*

# FOLLOW A RAINBOW ON OFFENSIVE LOBS

Are high-leaping opponents picking off too many of your offensive lob attempts? Chances are you've been trying to hit your lobs too perfectly, returning the ball on a trajectory that's too low to give you any margin of safety with the shot.

Even if you're able to catch an opponent at the net by surprise with your offensive lob, you must be sure to give the ball enough vertical lift to clear his raised racquet by a distance of at least a few feet.

That will be easier if you think of returning the ball on a rainbow-like trajectory over the net: Hit the ball so it arcs well above your opponent and lands deep near the baseline. Your offensive lob may not yield a pot of gold, but it could produce something else of value: a winning point.

*—Jack E. Seymore*

# LOB OVER THE BACKHAND

When playing an opponent who shows no respect for your passing shots and likes to camp a few feet from the net, there's nothing more enjoyable than unleashing a well-disguised offensive lob that sends him madly scrambling back for the ball.

Obviously, you can't go to the well too often for an offensive lob. But when you do let one fly, you'll improve your chances for success by aiming the shot over your opponent's backhand side. Of course, if your lob is deep enough, he won't be able to get his racquet on the ball.

But even if he's just able to reach the ball, he'll have to hit a backhand overhead—a tough shot for most players. He won't be able to put much power behind the shot, either, so you'll probably be able to take the offensive. Remember, make the backhand your target on offensive lobs to earn an opponent's respect.

—*Gary Horvath*

# LOB OVER THE GOALPOST FOR EXTRA POINTS

In football, teams score touchdowns by using a good blend of plays to keep their opponents guessing; they don't always go for the low-percentage long pass to a receiver streaking down the field.

Similarly, when your opponent is at the net in tennis, you shouldn't rely exclusively on a big passing shot to win the point outright. There are other options. And one of them is the offensive lob which, when hit properly, can win a number of extra points for you.

The next time an opponent takes command of the net, move in on a short shot and lift the ball high enough to clear his outstretched racquet. Imagine there's a football goalpost rising vertically above the opponent's service line. If you're able to stroke the ball high and deep enough to sail through the uprights and land near the baseline, you'll take the offense away from your opponent and score an extra point!

—*Bill Delaney*

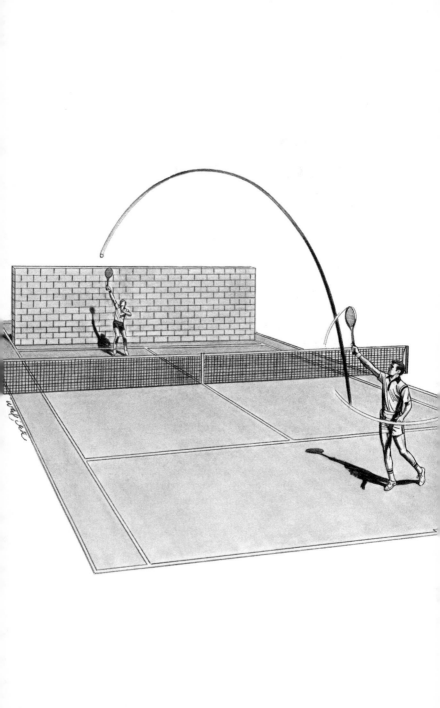

# LOB OVER AN IMAGINARY WALL

When your opponent is playing at the net and you hit a lob, whether offensive or defensive, you must be sure to place it high and deep enough in his backcourt to make it difficult for him to hit an effective overhead. One way to help you put this kind of trajectory on your lobs is to imagine that there's a wall just behind your opponent's service line. Visualize it as about 10 feet high—or about as high as the tip of your opponent's outstreched racquet if he were to jump for the ball at the service line. If you're able to lob the ball over this wall consistently, your shots will be deep enough to make his overheads more difficult and give you enough time to get into good position for returns.

—*Kenneth P. Wasserman*

# 5

# OVERHEADS

# "HANDS UP!" FOR BETTER OVERHEADS

That old cliche, "Hands up! Reach for the sky!" from Westerns and cops-and-robbers films, can be applied to help you hit better overheads. Here's how. As soon as you see your opponent lobbing the ball, turn sideways to the net and immediately raise both arms into the "Hands up!" position. That automatcially gets your hands working in unison and puts a rhythm in your swing.

From this ready position, you can easily continue your overhead stroking motion, dropping the racquet head down behind you and following the ball with your free hand. Then, when the ball comes into striking range, you should be able to pull the trigger and smash your overhead for a winner!

—*Joseph Kamrad*

# WAIT ON THE BALL FOR BETTER OVERHEADS

Has this ever happened to you? You're at the net and you've just forced an opponent to scramble wide of the court to retrieve a ball. When he sends up a weak, short lob, your eyes nearly pop out of your head as you anticipate an easy, putaway overhead. Only you blow the shot by rushing your swing.

Early racquet preparation is the key to preventing this problem. If you wait until the last second to whip the racquet around behind your back, especially in a service-type motion, you're more apt to mis-hit the ball. So I advise my students to lift their racquets up and back behind them as soon as the lob is hit, just like a waiter would lift a serving tray into carrying position over his shoulder. That early, simple preparation allows you to wait on the ball, make a smooth stroke and serve up a solid overhead.

—*Jim Kraus*

# HIT A SHADY OVERHEAD TO OVER-COME THE SUN

While it's great to play tennis outdoors in the summer, the elements can cause problems for the inexperienced player. The sun, for example, can be troublesome on a bright, cloudless day when you have to hit an overhead. It's easy to get blinded by the sun while tracking a lob.

How do you deal with that problem? As you turn sideways to the ball, make wise use of your free arm. Instead of tracking the ball until it disappears into the sun, position your hand and forearm like a parasol to block out the bright rays. That way, you'll be better able to follow the ball as it descends and hit a solid, winning overhead, instead of swinging blindly at the sunspots before your eyes. Hit a shady overhead and you'll see the ball in a better light.

*—Jim Turner*

# COCK YOUR ARM ON OVERHEADS LIKE THE HAMMER OF A GUN

When you find that you're mis-hitting a lot of overheads, the problem may be late racquet preparation. If your opponent sends up a lob and you don't begin lifting your racquet over your shoulder until the ball is well on its descent, you'll have to rush your swing.

The key to hitting solid overheads with consistency is to turn sideways to the net and lift your racquet up to prepare for the shot as soon as you can see a lob coming. It's like cocking the hammer of a gun. Without pulling back the hammer, you can't fire the pistol. Likewise, if you don't get your racquet up and back in time, you can't fire a clean overhead across the net.

*—Robert R. Myerson*

# HAMMER HOME YOUR OVERHEADS

The stroking motion involved in hitting an overhead is similar to the arm and hand movement used in hammering a nail above your head. When an opponent hits you a lob, take your racquet up and back behind you quickly, keeping your arm flexed and your wrist relaxed. Use a grip about halfway between your Eastern forehand and backhand grips, with your fingers spread slightly. As the ball comes into striking distance, swing the racquet upward swiftly, extend your arm completely and snap your wrist forward through impact in much the same way that a carpenter would drive a nail into a wooden plank. This motion will put more power behind your smashes and allow you to hammer them home for winners.

*—Ben Foster*

# ANGLE AWAY YOUR OVERHEADS

One of the most common traps club players fall into when hitting overheads is trying to pound the daylights out of the ball. By concentrating so much on power, though, they don't think about placement. The results are often overheads hit right back down the center of the court, allowing their opponents time to reach the ball.

If you want to increase your chances of hitting winning overheads, use court angles wisely. The closer you are to the net when you make contact with the ball, the more you'll be able to aim for angles toward the sidelines. And by going for such a placement, you won't have to hit the ball as hard because it will be angled away from your opponent. So when you're near the service line, don't play it straight on your overheads. Angle the ball away for a more direct winner.

—*Rick Macci*

# USE A SCISSORS KICK ON HIGH OVERHEADS

Although you've always been taught to hit your overheads with both feet planted firmly on the ground, there are times when you have to abandon that technique and jump to reach tough offensive lobs that you have no chance of running down.

In those cases, a scissors-like jump is the most efficient way of reaching the ball. Pivoting sideways, you should push backward, up off your back foot, to gain height off the ground and then land, after meeting the ball, on your other foot.

Viewed from the sideline, your legs would appear to move past each other like the blades of a pair of scissors. Of course, it's difficult to think about your footwork while you're stretching up to hit the ball. But when you land, you can check whether you're coming down on the proper foot. Use a scissors kick and you'll be able to cut off some of your opponent's offensive lobs.

*—Bill Delaney*

# SERVICE
# RETURNS

# REMEMBER THE THREE "R's" FOR BETTER SERVICE RETURNS

Do you have trouble hitting solid, consistent returns of serve? If so, you may be thinking of too many things at once as you execute the shot. Instead, you should go to school on the stroke by focusing your concentration on the three "R's" of service returns—ready, read and react—as your opponent gets set to make his delivery.

First, ready yourself for the serve by flexing your body and staying on your toes as the server lifts the ball into the air. Next, read his ball release and serving motion to get an idea of what type of serve he's going to deliver. And last, react by springing into action as soon as the ball leaves his racquet face so you're ready to hit a solid return. Remember, if you concentrate on your three "R's," you're sure to upgrade your service returns.

—*Bob Parker*

# USE A GOLFER'S WAGGLE TO PREPARE FOR SERVICE RETURNS

The "dead" time between points accounts for a large percentage of a tennis match's duration. Unfortunately, few players use this time of inactivity wisely. They'll glance at the court's surroundings, curse their luck or just daydream.

You should take advantage of this time, particularly when you're waiting to return serve, to practice your strokes and plan a return strategy. You should develop a routine like the golfer who waggles his club back and forth in a deliberate mini-stroke to preview his shot and check his club head's path and alignment. Make a few quick shoulder turns to each side, changing grips as you bring your racquet back. Then, move the racquet head through the contact area and check its alignment.

By waggling your racquet this way, you'll iron out the rough spots in your returns.

—*Joseph Kamrad*

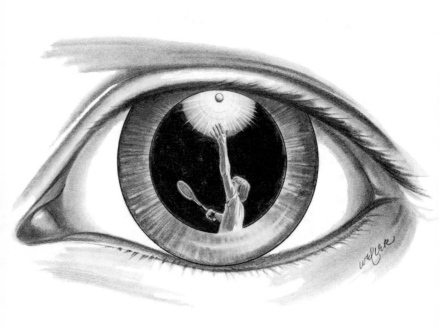

# FOCUS ON THE BALL EARLY FOR HAPPIER RETURNS

Many players mis-hit their service returns because they concentrate on the server's stroking motion rather than on the ball itself at the start of a point. As a result, they're late in getting a fix on the speed and direction of the ball, and then rush their swings. To overcome this problem, try focusing completely on the ball as your opponent prepares to serve. Make a point of observing it in his or her hand, watch it during the release and follow it intently as it leaves the racquet. By concentrating on the ball this way, you'll have more time to get set for the return and eliminate those rushed swings.

*—Fred Pinho*

# USE A WEDGE TO GET A SERVICE RETURN EDGE

Whoosh! A service ace flies past you. As soon as the ball left your opponent's racquet, you could see it was headed to your forehand side. You brought your racquet back early, yet your feet felt like they were mired in mud. What went wrong?

No, the clay court wasn't too wet. Most likely, you were simply standing flat-footed while waiting for the serve. Although your opponent enjoys an advantage when he serves, you can get a bit of an edge of your own if you stand prepared to spring into action.

Pretend that a wedge is pushed under your heels as you stand with your legs flexed in the ready position. That way, your weight will be transferred forward, onto the balls of your feet, just as the server is about to hit the ball. You'll be better able to pounce on his serves and perhaps, wedge a crucial service break from his grasp.

*—Michael E. Hurley*

# GET READY LIKE A QUARTERBACK

Because your opponent has the edge when he serves to start each point, you can't afford to be caught flat-footed near the baseline. You must be ready to move as soon as you see where the serve is heading.

In several ways, your ready position when you return serve should be similar to the stance a football quarterback assumes when he's preparing to take the snap at the line of scrimmage. He's got his weight on the balls of his feet, his knees are flexed and his hands are out in front of him. He's ready to spring into action, just as you should be.

The important difference is that a quarterback will retreat after the snap to hand off or to pass, while you should always try to move forward to return serve.

—*Tom Monahan*

# ON RETURNS, FLOAT LIKE A BUTTERFLY, STING LIKE A BEE

Many players have difficulty returning serve because they are standing flat-footed when their opponents deliver the ball. This stance prevents them from getting a quick jump on the ball and often results in forced, weak returns that can be put away easily.

If you keep getting burned that way on your returns of serve, heed the motto of boxing great Muhammad Ali and "float like a butterfly, sting like a bee." By staying on the balls of your feet and floating a la Ali, you'll be able to start for the ball more quickly, get into hitting position sooner and put more sting into your shots.

—*Mason Brunson*

# LEAN INTO THE WAVE WHEN RETURNING SERVE

Do you recall the first time you went to a beach as a child and the problems you faced when you tried to walk into the water? Remember how the waves pounding ashore would push you backward and almost knock you over if you didn't lean into them?

The lesson you learned so quickly on the beach can be applied to help sharpen your returns of serve on a tennis court, too, especially if you tend to think defensively when your opponents serve. Defensive thinking often leads you to lean backward as the ball approaches and results in weak returns that float across the net.

Instead, try to think of your opponent's serve as a wave that's breaking toward you. As you make your forward swing, lean into the shot just as you would to counteract the force of an oncoming wave. You'll get your weight behind your return and send the ball sailing solidly across the net.

*—Bob Parker*

# AIM FOR A NET-RUSHER'S FEET ON SERVICE RETURNS

Are you intimidated by aggressive serve-and-volleyers? Your problem may be that you know your service returns play a vital role against such opponents so you try to do too much with the ball by going for low-percentage, angled passing shots.

The next time you face a net-rusher, don't overlook one of the most effective return-of-serve targets—down the middle at the server's feet. This placement will allow you to hit the ball over the lowest part of the net and will give you plenty of court to work with. Most important, your opponent will find it tough to hit an offensive volley or half volley from below knee level. So remember to use the server's feet as a target on your returns against a net-rusher.

*—John P. Kelly*

# STEAL EXTRA TIME ON SERVICE RETURNS

Have you ever faced an opponent who drills serves so hard and fast to your backhand that you barely have time to adjust your grip on the racquet—let alone make a solid return?

The next time you have to deal with those cannonball deliveries, don't persist in holding your racquet with a forehand grip as so many players do when awaiting serve. Instead, try using a backhand grip.

That way, you won't have to change your grip to return serve as long as he continues to pound away at your backhand. You'll steal an extra split second of time to prepare for your return and probably steal a few points, too, when you begin to get the ball in play with greater regularity.

*—Steve J. Carpenter*

# 7
# SINGLES TACTICS

# BE A SMART GAMBLER ON COURT

When you play an important match, do you mentally keep track of an opponent's strategy? Or are you so nervous that you have your hands full concentrating on your own strokes?

Worrying about the technical aspects of your strokes will usually hurt you in a match. If you haven't perfected them in practice, you won't` under pressure. You will improve your chances of winning by paying attention to your opponent's shot-placement tendencies.

What are his favorite shots? In what situations? A top player will look for answers to these questions all the time. He's like a smart gambler on court; he can figure out an opponent's hand—his best shots—and counter them with his own strengths. If you can learn to play your cards right on court, too, it's a safe bet you'll win more matches.

—*Brice Bassett*

weiler

# TAKE A SHORT-CUT TO SHORT SHOTS

Are you forced to lunge desperately for the ball nearly every time an opponent angles a shot short into your forecourt? If you are, the problem, more than likely, is poor footwork on you r part. After the ball leaves your opponent's racquet, you probably take a few steps parallel with the baseline before realizing that the shot is going to land short. Then, you run in to intercept the ball. By that time, the ball has dropped too low to be returned aggressively.

To eliminate the problem, keep in mind a simple axiom of geometry: The shortest distance between two points is a straight line. React to your opponent's shots quickly and run toward the ball at an angle along that line. Or as your high school math teacher would put it: "Use the hypotenuse". It's your shortcut to success.

*—Jim Elgie*

# KEEP MOVING! DON'T PLANT YOUR FEET

Do you ever wish you could cover the court like Bjorn Borg or Vitas Gerulaitis, who were two of the fastest pros in the game? You can, even if you don't possess a lot of raw speed.

The secret is to follow an important fundamental of good footwork: Stay on your toes and move with your weight centered on the balls of your feet. The next time you watch quick pros play a match, notice how they keep their feet moving during a point, even when they're waiting for an opponent to hit a shot. You'll never see them wait for the ball with their feet firmly planted on the court.

That's the main reason why they're able to get such quick jumps on the ball. They keep their bodies poised and ready to spring in any direction. So whenever you slip into the habit of planting your feet during play, uproot yourself and move like a pro.

—*Chuck Sheftel*

# DON'T BE PUSHED AROUND! HIT ON THE RISE

Does your opponent seem to be able to move you around at will with heavy topspin ground strokes during baseline rallies? Under those conditions, it doesn't take long before you feel like a puppet on a string. You're repeatedly forced to return balls from deep behind your baseline without much offensive punch.

To fight back, move in and time your hit so that you make contact with the ball as it's rising after the bounce. Keep your swing simple and compact, since good timing is necessary when you hit on the rise. If you're successful, you'll be able to effectively use the pace of your opponent's shot to send back a solid return that won't allow him to enjoy a slow rallying pace.

What's more, you'll be closer to the baseline, or even inside it, which means you'll be able to hit more offensive shots. So remember to hit the ball on the rise if you want to lift the level of your play.

*—Don Harring*

# MOVE YOUR SERVES AROUND LIKE A BASEBALL PITCHER

The best pitchers in baseball have sufficient control to use every inch of the home plate's width in throwing to a batter. Varying the speed of their pitches, they move the ball inside and outside to keep hitters off stride.

That's the way you should try to serve in a tennis match, too. And it's not as hard as it might seem at first. After all, your home plate, the service court, is more than 13 feet wide (versus the 17-inch width of a home plate). To serve effectively, you should use all of that large area by mixing up the placement of your deliveries. Serve to the corners as well as down the middle and you'll keep your opponent guessing. It will be tough for him to strike back.

—Jim Price

# OBEY THE TRAFFIC LIGHT WHEN PLANNING TO ATTACK

Many club players become so physically and mentally engaged in long baseline rallies that they often overlook opportunities to rush the net to take command of a point. If you're one of these players, try this: Imagine that your half of the court is governed by a traffic light and that you have to obey its signals when you want to go on the attack.

When you're at or behind your baseline, the red light is on. You won't hit many winners from here, so concentrate instead on moving your opponent around and forcing a short return. When you're able to move in on a short ball and make contact between your baseline and service line, the yellow light is flashing. Stroke a deep approach shot, but use caution; you don't want to overhit the shot. Then, if your approach is solid, you have a green light to move up to the net and go for a winning volley from your forecourt.

Remember to wait for the green light before you go to the net to stop a lot of opponents.
—*Chris Maytnier*

# HIT DOWN THE LINE WHEN PULLED WIDE

When an opponent hits an angled shot that pulls you wide of the court—but not so wide that you have to scramble frantically to reach the ball and send up a lob—you should consider a down-the-line placement.

Why? In running down a wide return, it's often difficult to meet the ball early enough in your swing to hit a solid crosscourt shot without using a lot of wrist action. And if your shot is weak, your opponent will have a wide-open court into which he can stroke a clean winner.

By hitting down the line, though, you can keep the action more or less in front of you. And you should be in a good position to cover any down-the-line return. What's more, an aggressive down-the-line shot may force a weak return that you can capitalize on immediately. So don't automatically think "defense" when you're pulled wide; stroke the ball aggressively down the line and you may be able to turn the point around.

*—Paul Gagon*

# SHIFT STROKING GEARS TO KEEP OPPONENTS OFF BALANCE

Do you have trouble beating baseliners who blast one powerful ground stroke after another at you? If you do, you may be falling into their pattern of play by trying to match their power, stroke for stroke.

To keep these power players off balance, you should mix up your attack during baseline rallies—much as you shift gears in your car to control your speed. Instead of becoming engaged in slugfests you have little chance of winning, shift stroking gears occasionally on court. Throw in some slice strokes, too, to take the pace off the ball and force your opponent to generate all of the power on his own. That can throw off his timing and balance, as well as tire him in the long run.

So gear your stroking attack to win; become a shifty player on court.

—*Howard Schroeder*

# COMPRESS A SPRING WHEN RUSHING THE NET

Rushing the net during a point is an aggressive move designed to put you in a strong offensive position in your forecourt. But if you're an inexperienced net-rusher, you may find yourself so intent upon moving forward and closing out the point that you overlook the possibility your opponent may catch you off guard with a deep lob until it's too late.

A good way to spare yourself that frustration is to imagine that you're compressing a giant spring between yourself and the net as you move forward. The more a spring is compressed, remember, the faster it will uncoil. The same principle applies to your net-rushing: the quicker and closer you get to the net, the more prepared you must be to spring quickly back to cover a lob return.

*—Gregg Kail*

# APPROACH WITH CAUTION!

How often in your matches do you move in on a short ball from an opponent and drive it long, beyond his baseline? If that's a persistent problem for you, you're trying to do too much with the ball; in your eagerness to win a point, you're overhitting your approach shots. You must remember your purpose in hitting an approach shot: to set up a winning volley at the net, not to take the point outright. So use caution when you move in to intercept a short ball. Maintain your balance and swing smoothly. Stroke the ball deep but at about three-quarter speed to be sure that your shot will land in the court and force a return. Then, you can proceed to the net and hit a volley for a winner!

—*Hugh Curtler*

# LET A TAIL WIND CARRY YOU TO THE NET

No one likes playing tennis in a gusty wind that swirls unpredictably around the court. But a steady tail wind is another matter. You can use it to your advantage by advancing to the net and volleying aggressively when the wind's at your back. That's because a tail wind will measurably slow down your opponent's passing shot attempts, giving you more time to reach the ball and volley it back firmly. Remember, though, don't overhit the ball at the net or the tail wind will carry it long. And finally, beware of a lob from your opponent. He'll be able to loft the ball higher and deeper because the wind will blow it back into the court.

—*Ben Foster*

# AIM AT THE NET PLAYER'S HIP

When players are engaged in a volleying battle at the net, especially in doubles, they sometimes become overly obsessed with the idea of punching the ball *past* their opponents. So much so, in fact, that they often neglect one of the most effective shots they can use against a volleyer—a drive aimed directly at the racquet side of the player's body, between the hip and armpit.

You've probably faced one of these shots. How did you return it? Remember the way you had to defend yourself with a quick, backhand blocking motion? You couldn't put anything on the shot, could you? That's precisely the reason why you should always keep a volleyer's racquet side in mind as a target for solid shots. You'll often handcuff an opponent and force a defensive shot.

*—Gary Horvath*

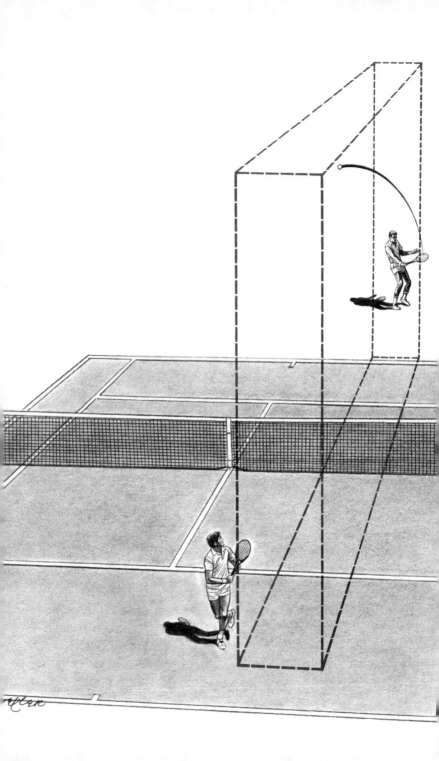

# USE AN IMAGINARY ALLEY WHEN CHASING LOBS

One of the most common mistakes players make when running down deep lobs is to retreat directly beneath the path of the ball. What happens? When the ball bounces, they're usually too close to take a full, normal swing. They either have to take a quick step away from the ball or lean backward from it, forcing a rushed, tightly cramped hitting motion. And the result, of course, is a weak, ineffective return.

The next time an opponent lofts a deep lob over your head, run down the shot quickly but move in a direction *parallel* with the ball's line of flight. Imagine that there's an alley (about the width of the one between sidelines on a tennis court) between you and the path of the ball as you retreat. That way, you should be in fine position to make a strong return when the ball lands.

—*Larry Abrams*

# DOUBLES
# TACTICS

# HUDDLE FOR BETTER DOUBLES

Doubles partners who fail to communicate with each other during a match are like a football team that tries to run complex plays without calling a huddle. They can't work together the way they should and the results will show it.

Often, in fact, partners who don't talk strategy are usually out of points before they begin. That's because they're always on the defense, merely reacting to shots that the opposing team fires across the net.

If you and your doubles partner both have sound strokes, but frequently lose matches to less talented opponents, you're probably not communicating enough and working together as a team with an offensive plan. For better results, talk to each other briefly about your strategy between points. Call a huddle to score more often.

—*Jim Lathrop*

# MOVE LIKE WINDSHIELD WIPERS IN DOUBLES

To win consistently at doubles, you and your partner have to move on court as a team—in much the same fashion as a set of synchronized windshield wipers. Just as wipers clean a maximum area of glass without interfering with each other, so should you and your partner move in unison to cover your halves of the court effectively.

For example, when one of you is pulled wide by a shot, the other should move in the same direction to cover the opening down the middle. And if you hit a ball into one of the alleys, you and your teammate should move toward that side to cut off the angles of return. Remember, the team that moves well together usually wins doubles matches—and wipes its opponents off the court!

—*Paul Gagon*

# FACE THE NETMAN WHEN YOUR PARTNER IS RECEIVING SERVE IN DOUBLES

It's your partner's turn to receive serve in a doubles game and you take your position near your service line. Do you square off to face the net and server directly in front of you? If you do, you're hurting your team's chances on the point.

As the receiver's partner, your initial assignment is to protect your half of the court if the service return goes to the opposing netman and he then volleys the ball sharply toward you. To be prepared for that, try facing the netman, not the server and the net. That way, you should be able to pivot and move more easily to cover volleys hit to either side of you. Then, when you see that your partner's return will not be hit by the netman, you should square off to face the advancing server and deal with his first volley.

—*Nolie S. Howard*

# CROSS-STEP LIKE A BASERUNNER WHEN POACHING

Poaching in doubles—that is, moving laterally at the net to cut off an opponent's return—demands quick, decisive action. Just like a baseball player who must commit himself to steal second base, the netman who decides to poach can't change his mind and reverse direction when he sees he won't be able to reach the ball.

Because poaching is an offensive tactic, you must move forcefully to intercept the ball. So rather than sidestepping carefully crosscourt, you should pivot and cross-step aggressively with your outside leg (the one nearest the sideline) to get all of your weight moving quickly in the proper direction—just as a baserunner does to steal a base. Remember, once you've made a commitment to poach, there's no turning back. Run to pick off the ball in mid-air and steal the point!

—*Paul Gagon*

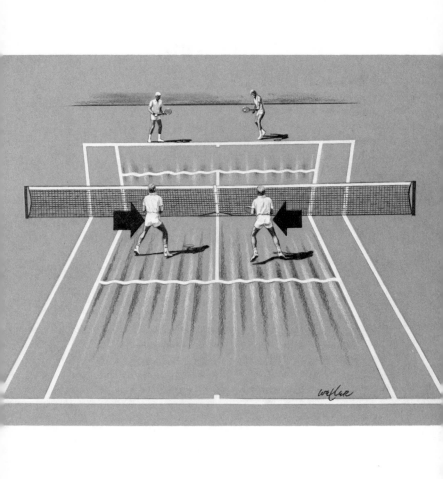

# SQUEEZE THE MIDDLE IN DOUBLES

In typical club doubles play, a net player who gets passed by a shot down the alley usually starts inching toward the sideline to make sure he doesn't get burned again. By doing that, though, he makes the middle of the court more vulnerable to attack. The effects can be devastating—especially since the center of the court is the major target area in doubles.

To keep the percentages in your favor, you and your partner should squeeze in slightly toward the middle of the court. That way, you'll not only cover the largest area of your court that's likely to come under attack; you'll also force your opponents to attempt riskier down-the-line passing shots. So remember to squeeze the middle to put pressure on opponents.

*—Don Harring*

# DRIVE DOWN THE MIDDLE IN DOUBLES

One of the wisest, but perhaps most over-looked tactics in doubles play is to return balls between your opponents down the middle of the court. The heat of battle may tempt you to go for a lot of angled winners, but there's no better road to doubles success than the opening that separates the opposing team.

Consider the advantages of going that route. First, you're hitting over the lowest part of the net. Second, you're cutting down your opponents' angles of return. And third, your placement can cause confusion because the other team must decide in a split second which one is going to hit the ball.

So the next time you find yourself in a heated doubles rally, try driving the ball down the road between your opponents. They'll find it tough to stop your momentum.

—*Paul Gagon*